MY BOOK

OF

FABLES

Great Selection of Simple and Interesting Fables for All Ages

R. Lopz

TABLE OF CONTENTS

Introduction

I want to thank and congratulate you for downloading the book, "My Book of Fables".

This book contains of perfect collection of simple, interesting and lovely Fables for not just for kids but for all ages. This book is full of surprises and I am sure that all of you will enjoyed the book.

This is a great read before bedtime. Full of great little fables that will brings and give all you awesome information and ideas that your kids will surely be loved.

After reading this book, you will know and find out some new ideas and interesting things about different kinds of animals that is perfect for your family and friends, especially for your kids.

Thanks again for downloading this book. I hope you enjoy it!

Wolf and a Crane

A greedy wolf ate in a great hurry and got a bone struck in it's throat. It pleaded with a crane to remove it, promising some reward.

The crane willingly helped the wolf and later demanded for it's reward. But the cunning and ungrateful wolf did not fullfill it's promise. It said that sparing crane's head was reward enough.

The Bee and the Bull

There once lived a conceited bee. It was quite fussy, too. One day. after a long flight, it decided to stop and rest. The place it choose was the horn of a bull that was gazing in a nearby field.

Swooping down, it landed on the bull's horn. Clearing it's throat, it said, "I hope I am not too heavy for you, sir. If so, just tell meand I'll be on my way."

"As you please, little one," said the bull. "But to tell you the truth, I didn't even know that you were there. So I definitely won't notice when you go."

A Lion In Love

A lion fell in love with a country maid and asked her father if he could marry her. Though the father was frightened, he kept his cool. He said that his daughter was a foolish girl who was so afraid of the lion's sharp teeth and claws.

He said that his dauhghter will marry the lion if he had his claws and teeth removed. The lion agreed. He went to the dentist and had his teeth pulled out and his claws removed.

The next moment, the father killed the lion with a cudgel.

An Old Man and an Ass

An old man and his young son were walking along with an ass that they plan to sell. A passerby laughed at them because they were walking beside the beast of burden instead of riding it. So the man made his on the ass.

Further on, a traveler scolded his son for making his old father walk. At this, the son got off and made his father sit on the ass. Still futher on, another person expressed disbelief at the father sitting on the ass while his young son walked.

Finally, the father and son carried the ass on their shoulders. This amused everyone.

The Ox and the Frog

A young frog lived very contentedly till one day it stepped out of it's pool. It saw a huge ox in the nearby meadow. It started envying the big size of the ox.

In an attempt to become as large as the ox, the frog took in lots of air to puff itself up. It then compared it's size to that of the ox. There was still a huge difference.

Getting annoyed at the slow progress, it breathed deeper and faster, till it puffed itself up so much that it finally burst.

The Little Pine Tree

A little pine tree had green needles all year round and yet it wasn't happy. It wanted leaves of gold. The wish was granted. But a man came and plucked them all.

It next thought that leaves of grass were the best, and once more the wish was granted. But the wind came and all he glass leaves broke. Next it wishes for green leaves. These were all eaten by a goat.

The little pine tree realized that it was best to be satisfied with what one has.

The Golden Goose

One day, a fairy rewarded a woman for her hard work. The woman receives a golden goose. Each day the goose would lay a golden egg.

The woman would sell the egg and buy things she wanted.

But soon the woman got greedy and wanted all the treasure at once. She cut the goose to get all the eggs only to find that there were none inside.

Two Cocks at Quarrel

Two cocks fought to be he master of poultry yard. When the duel was over, the victor crowed and clapped it's wings in great delight.

It made so much noise that an eagle passing swooped down and carried it away. Now the entire yard belonged to the defeated cock.

An Old Lion

There once lived a lion who was very cruel in his youth. So when he became old and in not so good form, most of the beasts in the forest treated him badly. Some insulted him, other's laughed at him and still other's took revenge on him.

He was a miserable creature towards the end of his days. But nothing hurt him more deeply in his time of sorrow and ashamed off than to find himself battered by thee heel of an ass.

A Country Mouse and a Town Mouse

Once there were two mice. One lived in the country and the other lived in a town. The country mouse invited the town mouse for dinner and served him the best food. But the town mouse said that the food was tasteless and invited the country mouse to his house.

At the town mouse's house, the food was very tasty. But all the time, while they were eating, the town mouse was on lookout for human beings and cats they kept to kill mice.

"What a miserable life you lead!" exclaimed the country mouse. "Back, in the country, at least I can eat my meals in peace. Thanks for your hospitality but I think I would like to go back home.

A Dog in a Manger

A dog happened to stay into a cowshed while searching for food. It climbed on the pile of hay in he manger and sniffed at it, hoping to find something to eat. It was hungry and tired that it laid on the hay. But it hated the taste and could not bring itself to eat it.

When the cow came to the cowshed and saw the dog, it said, "Please get off the manger. I want to eat my meal." The dog snarled at the cow and refused to move. Even though it could not eat the hay, it refused to get up and let the cow have it's meal.

A Boot in the Jungle

"I am sure it's the shell of a fruit," said the bear, looking at a boot he found in the jungle.

"Rubbish!" said the wolf. "It's a nest. Here is the hollow in which the bird lays it's eggs."

"Foolish!" said the parrot, pointing to the long laces. "It's a plant. See, here are thee roots."

A monkey who was listening to their arguments, said that it was a boot and that it had seen men wearing such things on their feet.

The other animals laughed at the mnonkey, saying that they definitely had never seen men wearing such thing.

A Monkey and A Crocodile

Everyday, a monkey would eat a mango and give two to a crocodile. Of these, one was for the crocodile's wife thought that since the mangoes everyday, his heart would be tasty, too. She asked her husband to invite the monkey home so that she could eat his heart. The crocodile did so reluctantly. On their way, he told the monkey the reason of invitation.

The monkey said that he had left his heart on a mango tree and that if the crocodile would allow him to go back, he would bring it with him. As soon as the crocodile took him ashore, the monkey bade the crocodile goodbye!

A Stag and it's Antlers

A stag was drinking at a pool. It looked at it's reflection and remarked, "I have such glorious antlers but my leg are so thin!"

Just then, the stag heard some hunters rushing towards the pool. It fled in terror. It's slender legs carried it swiftly away from danger.

Once inside the thick forest, it thought that it was safe. But antlers, which it valued so much, proves to be it's enemy. They got entangled in the branches and no matter how hard it struggled, it could not get free. And very soon the hunters tracked it down and trapped it.

The Dog and the Bone

A dog sat chewing at a delicious bone that it had found near the river. It chewed the bone for a very long time and soon this made it quite thirsty. It decided to go to the river to quench it's thirst. It took the bone along as it was worried that some other dog might take it away.

As it stood near the river, it saw it's reflection in the water. It seemed o see another dog with a bone in his mouth. And being greedy by nature, it wanted that bone too. So it barked at the other dog, hoping to scare it and give the bone to him. But atlas! The bone that it held in it's mouth fell into the river.

A Fox and a Stork

Once a fox invited a stork to dinner and served it some soup in a flat dish. Though it knew very well that the stork, with it's long break, could not feed from the flat dish, it said, "I hope you're enjoying the tasty meal I prepared." The stork merely looked on helplessly and so the fox lapped up it's share, too.

After a few days, the stork invited the fox to dinner and served it food in a jug with a long and narrow neck. The fox realized that it was being repaid for it's rude behavior with the stork.

A Young Crab and her Mother

A mother crab, quite particular about her daughter's grooming, was very concerned at her crooked manner of walking. But no matter how hard she tried, the daughter was not successful in walking straight.

One day, tired and disappointed, the young crab said, "Mother, I've tried and tried, but with no success. Please, why don't you show me how to walk straight."

"Sure, this is how to do it," said the mother, as she walked a short strech and in a crooked line.

A Lion and a Rabbit

A lion said to the animals in the forest that if one of them came out to him as his meal for the day, he would not kill any one of them. The animals agreed to this.

One day it was the rabbit's turn and it took very long time before reaching the lion. It said that it was stopped by another lion, who claimed to be the king of the jungle. "And he wants to meet you, your lordship." "So do I!" said the furious lion.

The rabbit took the lion to a well and showed it it's reflection. The lion jumped into jumped into the wellto chase it's opponent and got drowned.

A Hunter and a Rabbit

A hunter once caught a rabbit and was carrying it home for his meal. After trying very hard to escape, the rabbit said to the hunter, "If you let me go. I'll show you where the rest of my companions are hidden, and so your catch will grow larger."

"No," said the hunter, "now you surely shall die, for having been so eager to betray your friends!"

A Horse and a Stag

A wild horse was gazing on a grassy land, which it had all to itself. After a while it saw a stag come and nibble on the same grassland. The horse did not like sharing the grass and so it wanted to get rid of the stag. It told a man about it's plan and asked him if he would help it kill the stag.

The man agreed to the horse's plan, but said that to achieve this, he would have to mount the horse in order to chase the stag. The horse submitted to this and very soon the man killed the stag. But once he ahd done this, he refuses to alight from the horse's back and maed it his own beast of burden.

The Discontented Dog

A dog saw a cat on a high wall and wished it could be up there. But it ccould not climb. Then it saw a fish in the pond so that it would be cooler, just then it heard the fish say that it wished it too could lie on the green grass; and it heard the bird say that it wished it had the comforts that the dog had.

Hearing this, the dog realized that it should be contented with what it had.

An Ant and a Pigeon

An ant slipped into the water while drinking from a brook and was nearly drowned. A pigeon saw this happen and being kind-hearted, it threw the ant a little twig.

The ant climbed onto it and saved itself. A little later, the ant saw a hunter take aim at the pigeon. It ran up to the hunter and bit him hard on the leg. This made the hunter lose his aim and the pigeon flew away to safety.

The Foolish Chicken

One day a chicken stood near a pond watching the ducks swim past. It longed to swim like them. But it's mother warned it not to go near the pond, as it would fall into the water and drown.

Yet, wanting to be like the ducks, it dived into the pond, and then it was too late. The poor chicken drowned.

The Cat and the Mice

A large number of mice lived in a garden. They loved the garden because there was a grocer's store near it. They fed on the grain, cheese and biscuit in his store.

In the same garden lived a cat. It caught the mice whenever it could and made a meal of them.

The mice called a meeting to tackle the cat problem and decided to hang a bell around it's neck. That way, whenever the cat came close they would be warned.

Now came the question of who would bell the cat. Not a single mouse was brave enough. And so they had to endure the cruel cat.

Two Burden Asses

Two asses were crossinga shallow river with huge burdens on their backs.

While crossing the river, the ass that was ahead lost it's balance and fell down in the river. When it got up and walked again it's load seemed lighter. The second ass saw this and imitated the first ass. But when it stood up it's load had become even heavier.

Actually the first ass was carrying salt that dissolved in the water and so it's burden lightened. But the seconf ass was carrying cotton that soaked up water from the river and as a result it's load became even more difficult to carry.

The Snake and the Mice

Snakes, as you know are cruel by nature. At times they like to hurt others without any reason.

Once upon a time, a snake got into a knife shop. It saw many sharp and gleaming knives there. It started licking one that attracted it the most.

Soon it saw blood on the knife and got excited. It licked the knife even more and saw more blood on the knife. Little did the foolish snake know that it was it's own tongue that bled.

After a while, the snake started feeling tired and faint and before it knew what was happening, it fell down unconscious.

The Oak and the Willow

An oak tree and a willow tree grew side by side on the banks of a river. One day, a storm came and the trees had a difficult time standing straight. The oak tree was having a more difficult time than the willow. The willow tree advised the oak tree to bend a little, along with the wind, saying that it would be easier to tackle the strong wind in this way. But that was against the oak tree's nature.

When the storm ended the mighty oak tree had been knocked down while the willow tree still stood firmly. The oak tree wondered why?

The willow tree replied. "I am only a humble tree. So when the wind blew, I bent with it. That is why I am still here.

The Crow and the Pitcher

It was a hot summer day. A crow was looking arounnd for water to quench it's thrist. It could not find any water anywhere. It was so hot that all rivers and lakes and pools had dried up.

At last it spotted a broken earthenware pitcher. The crow flew down and landed on the neck of the pitcher was so low that it could not reach it.

Suddenly an idea flashed across it's mind. It picked up some pebbles that were lying nearby and dropped them into the pitcher. Slowly, the water level rose. The crow drank till it's thrist was quenched and then flew away.

Two Foolish Goats

While crossing a narrow log bridge, two goats came face to face with each other. Neither wanted to give way to the other. So they started fighting and fell into the stream below.

The next day two other goats were faced with the same problem. But these goats were not foolish. One sat down while the other stepped over it's body. The goat that crossed first thanked the other goat and promised to let it pass the next time they were faced with the same problem.

A Bear and some Bees

On a hot sunny afternoon, a bear was sleeping peacefully in a shade of a leafy mango tree. A bee that was passing by envied he bear and decided to sting it. Just as it was stung the bear woke up. It was so angry that it decided to knock down all he beehives in revenge.

The bees could not bear to teach it a lesson. The bear got badly stung.

It said itself, "It would have been wiser for me to let one injury pass tan to receive so many."

A Fox and a Goat

It was a hot day. A fox and a goat were looking for water to quench their thrist. Finally, they came upon a well that had very little water.

So they climbed down the well and had their fill. When they quenched their thrist, the goat panicked. "How are we going to get out of the well?" it asked.

"Don't worry," replied the fox. "Just help me climb out. Then I'll pull you out."

The goat very innocently did what he was told. But once the fox was out it did not bother about the goat and went away quietly.

An Honest Woodcutter

A woodcutter accidentally dropped his axe into a river. He just could not afford to buy another one. He stood helplessly beside the river when a fairy appeared and held out an axe made out of gold to him.

The woodcutter did not take it as it did not belong to him. His honestly did not allow him to take the axe made of silver either, which the fairy tempted him with. Finally, the fairy held out an axe with a wooden handlle.

"That's mine. Thank you!" smiled the woodcutter. Seeing his honestly, the fairy gave him all the three axes.

The Ant and the Grasshopper

On a warm summer day, a grasshopper was singing in the garden. It laughed at the ant which was busy gathering and storing away food for the winter. The ant told the grasshopper to do the same but it scoffed at the ant.

Winter came. The snow fell and covered everything. There were no leaves in sight. The grasshopper was so hungry but it had nothing to eat. As the days passed by the grasshopper's condition became worse. It was almost dying of starvation.

It then decided to appeal to the ant for help, but the ant shut the door saying, "You sang in the summer; now dance the winter away!"

The Raven and the Swan

A raven was so envy of the swan because of it's flawless fair skin.

It's desire to be as white and as beautiful as the swan grew everyday. The problem is it does not know how to make itself white.

One day, an idea flashed across it's mind. It thought, "The swan keeps bathing itself again and again. Maybe that's why it's so white. Yes, I'll also bathe myself endlessly till I become as white as the swan."

It did exactly that. The raven rubbed and scrubbed itself day after day until it got tired. Unfortunately, all it got was a cold and the bitter truth that it could never be as fair as the swan.

A Fox and some Grapes

A fox kept licking it's lips as it stood at a cluster of grapes that hung on a wall. It then jumped up to get the grapes but they were beyond it's reach.

It tried many times with no luck. Finally getting weary, it went way saying that the grapes were sour!

An Ass, A Lion and a Cock

A cock and an ass were sitting under a tree sharing a meal when a lion spotted them.

"How perfect!" said the lion. "I don't need to hunt far and wide. Under the tree sits my next meal."

Seeing the lion, he cock flew on a branch and crowed in fear. The strange sound frightened the lion and it fled.

The ass, thinking that the lion was frightened, started chasing the lion. Little did the stupid animal realized that it was the cock's crow that had scared the lion. The lion suddenly stopped and turned upon the ass. After a while, the lion tore the ass into pieces.

A Wold in Sheep's Clothing

A cunning wolf could not penetrate the sheep pen no matter how hard it tried. A farmer was always on guard keeping a careful watch. One day, it disguised itself as a sheep. It wrapped itself with sheepskin.

It crept into the flock and waited for the right moment to catchone for it's meal. The alert farmer saw the thief among his flock.

He hung him up, sheepskin and all, as an spectacle and an example.

A Fox and a Crow

A fox saw a crow upon a tree with a morsel in it's beak. The fox thought of a cunning way to get it's food. The flattered the crow for it's good singing voice.

The crow was foolish enough to believe what the fox said and started singing. The bit of food that it held in it's beak fell to the ground. The fox hurriedly picked it up and ate it.

"I may have praised your voice, but I said nothing about your brain!" it said.

A Lion and a Mouse

One day a mosue got trapped under the paw of a lion. The mouse pleaded for it's life. Being generous by nature, the lion set it free. The mouse promised to help the lion if it got the chance. The lion laughed at this. After all how could a tiny mouse help the king of the jungle?

A few days later, the mouse was passing through the jungle when it saw the samw lion trapped in a hunter's net.

At once it set to work, gnawing at the ropes. Very soon the tiny mouse had set the lion free and was very thankful to his tiny friend.

Conclusion

Thanks again for downloading "My Book of Fables": Great Selection of Simple and Interesting Fables for All Ages .

I hope this book will help you to have some additional ideas and information about different kinds of animals that is perfect for your family and friends, especially for your kids. This is a great read before bedtime. Full of great little fables that will brings and give all you awesome information and ideas that your kids will surely be loved.

Finally, if you enjoyed the book, please take a little time to share your thoughts and post a simple and honest review on Amazon. It will be greatly appreciated!

Again, thanks for downloading and I hope that you enjoyed reading this book.

THANK YOU SO MUCH!!!!

R. Lopz